DRAGON GIRLS

Mina the Lightning Dragon

by Maddy Mara

Scholastic Inc.

ISBN 978-93-5954-461-8

First printing 2024
This reprint edition May 2026
Book design by Cassy Price

Printed in India at Shivam Offset Press, New Delhi

Mina was sitting at the kitchen table on her mom's laptop, playing a game. She smiled as she watched three avatars flying through a lush forest. Mina was the one dressed in silver. The one in black was Hana, her twin sister. In the middle was an avatar wearing purple. That was Zora, the twins' cousin.

The three girls loved spending time together but they didn't get the chance to do so very often. Zora lived on the other side of the country. Just recently the three girls had all attended their grandma's eightieth birthday party. That had been so much fun. But now they wouldn't see each other for months and months.

Luckily, they could still meet up in online games. *Magic Treasure Zone* was one of their favorites. You had to search for hidden treasures while constantly avoiding danger. It was exciting to play and took a lot of skill.

Mina got better each time they played the game. She loved flying through the imaginary world. But the best part about the game was chatting with the others. Right now, Hana was upstairs in their bedroom, on the computer the twins shared. Zora was in her room, thousands of miles away. Even though they were apart, it felt like they were together.

Outside, lightning flashed. Mina typed a message into the game's chat. *There's a storm coming!*

Zora replied: *There's one coming here, too. I just saw lightning.*

Mina felt a tingling in her spine. Of course, it wasn't impossible for there to be a storm in two parts of the country at the same time. It must happen sometimes.

But something else had happened to the cousins recently. Something that definitely didn't happen very often. The three girls had been drawn into a realm called the Magic Forest. And that wasn't even the most exciting part. Once they were there, Mina, Hana, and Zora transformed into magnificent dragons. They weren't just any type of dragon, either. They were Storm Dragons!

Hana was the Thunder Dragon. This made perfect sense to Mina. Her twin was loud and bold. Mina was the Lightning Dragon, but she wasn't sure yet what her special powers were. In dragon form, Mina had a lightning bolt on her forehead. And everyone always said she was as fast as lightning. But Mina didn't really care what her special power was. Being a Storm Dragon was amazing, no matter what!

Outside, lightning flashed again. This time it lit up the entire night sky.

Whoa! wrote Zora. *We just had a MASSIVE strike here.*

So did we, typed Hana. *Something is going on. I can feel it.*

The tingling up Mina's back grew stronger. The Tree Queen, the ruler of the Magic Forest, had told them they would see a storm when it was time to return to her. The girls had completed one task for the queen, but there was more to be done.

Mina heard the faint hum of a song. Was it coming from the computer?

Magic Forest, Magic Forest, come explore . . .

Mina's excitement swelled. She'd heard this song just before she went to the Magic Forest last time. Now she was sure of it—they were being called back!

Mina started typing a message. But something odd happened. The keyboard vanished. Mina blinked. The screen was getting bigger and brighter by the second.

Magic Forest, Magic Forest, come explore . . .

The song grew louder. It came from all around her. Lightning flashed outside and the window flew open. The room filled with swirling wind and the air smelled like ripe mangoes and cinnamon. On the computer, the forest trees stretched up and out of the screen until they surrounded Mina. Now she could hear the rustling of leaves and smell rich forest soil.

Lightning flashed again and the air crackled with electricity. Mina shut her eyes as the sweet-scented wind swirled around her, lifting her out of her seat. From somewhere nearby she heard the final line from the song.

Magic Forest, Magic Forest, hear my roar!

Mina felt herself plop gently back down as the wind died away. But she didn't land on the chair. Beneath her she could feel soft grass.

I'm back in the Magic Forest! she thought, her heart beating fast.

Mina blinked open her eyes. Everything was dark except for a mysterious pale green glow.

The only noise was the faint rustling of the trees.

Something's not right. Mina could feel it in the air.

A strange static noise rose up, crackling louder and louder. A glowing bolt of green ripped across the sky. Lightning! Usually Mina loved lightning. In her opinion, it was the most exciting part of a storm.

But this was no ordinary lightning. It was acid green, for one thing. And rather than making a zigzag across the sky, this lightning traced out a confused, tangled scrawl like a toddler's drawing.

Mina's stomach clenched. Last time they were in the Magic Forest, there'd been a problem with the thunder. The Chaos Queen and her critters had stolen part of the Thunder Maker. Luckily, Mina, Hana, and Zora had managed to fix it.

"It looks like the Chaos Queen is messing with the lightning now," Mina said aloud.

"You're right, Storm Dragon!" said a large insect that was fluttering next to Mina.

It was the most interesting bug Mina had ever seen. Its sleek body looked like it was made from shiny metal. "You look like a dragon!" Mina said.

The insect gave a snorty sort of laugh, sending out tiny plumes of smoke. "Of course I do," she said in a surprisingly loud voice. "Haven't you ever met a dragonfly?"

"I have," Mina said, thinking about the dragonflies in the park near her home. "But I've never met one like you. You seem special."

The dragonfly fluttered her wings proudly. "Why, thank you! My name is Gleami. I've come to take you to the Tree Queen's glade. It's dark in the forest, as you've probably noticed. But my wings generate light so I can guide your way. We'll have to watch out for Chaos Critters. They are furious that you Storm Dragons outsmarted them last time. They've been awaiting your return, Lightning Dragon."

Despite this bad news, Mina couldn't help smiling. She loved being called the Lightning Dragon!

"Come on, let's go," said Gleami, rising into the air and zipping off between the trees. A warm haze of purple light shone out around the little dragonfly, lifting the gloom wherever she went.

Mina stretched out her wings and launched into the air. Mina, Hana, and Zora had taken to flying instantly. Hana said it was because they did so much virtual flying in *Magic Treasure Zone*. Mina agreed. But flying in the Magic Forest was way more fun than flying online. She loved weaving between the trees, surging faster with each flap of her powerful wings. Being a Dragon Girl was amazing!

The wind brushed against her shimmery scales as she followed Gleami. The farther they went, the darker the forest became. Mina was glad to have the comforting glow of the dragonfly to follow. The forest was so quiet! Mina couldn't hear a single bird singing or animal foraging. The only sounds were the high-speed buzz of Gleami's wings and the slower flap of her own.

Mina cocked her head. *Hang on*... Now she could hear something. It was a scratchy, scuttling sound. *What is it?*

Then came the strange crackling noise she'd heard before, followed by another bolt of tangled green lightning. When it lit up the surrounding trees, Mina yelped. The trees were full of beady little eyes, all fixed on her.

"Chaos Critters!" Mina yelled. "Gleami, look out!"

A terrible screeching filled the air as the critters swarmed along the branches toward Mina. She could hear their sharp claws scratching on the bark.

Shuddering, Mina sped up. She had a horrible feeling that she knew what the critters were planning. Sure enough, the dark shapes began leaping from the branches. They hovered in midair before landing on her back and wings.

"Hey!" Mina cried.

The nasty little things were nipping at her! Her strong dragon scales protected her, but she didn't like this one bit. Were the critters trying to stop her from flying? If so, it was having the opposite effect. There was no way these creatures were going to slow down Mina.

She shook herself hard, still flying at full speed. She managed to throw off quite a few critters. But Mina could feel that plenty of others still clung to her. She frowned. She did not want to give these horrible creatures a free ride!

Mina looked around the gloomy forest, searching for an idea. Then it struck her. She needed something to scrape off the critters!

Mina saw two trees growing close together. There was just enough space for her to squeeze between them. At least, she hoped there was. *There's one way to find out!*

Clamping her wings tightly to her sides, Mina shot into the narrow gap between the trees, spiraling like a torpedo as she went. She felt the roughness of the sturdy tree trunks rubbing against her scales.

The Chaos Critters screeched as they were scraped from Mina's back and wings, tumbling away into the darkness.

Mina straightened up and stretched out her wings again. Gleami caught up with her, glowing brighter than ever. "Well done, Mina! You handled that like a total pro. And just in time. Look, we're at the Tree Queen's glade."

Mina gazed at the shimmering air that protected the glade. Through the haze she could faintly see a gorgeous garden. Unlike the rest of the forest, the glade was bathed in warm light, making it look more beautiful than ever. Mina's heart leapt when she spotted two familiar dragon shapes. Hana and Zora were already in there!

She turned to her new dragonfly friend. "Thanks for leading me here, Gleami. And thanks for your help with those Chaos Critters."

Gleami did a quick, shiny loop, snorting smoke into the air. "It was my honor, Lightning

Dragon," she said. "The moment you need me again, I'll return to your side."

Gleami soared through the air in an arc, her wings shimmering like jewels, before zipping away between the trees.

Mina took a deep breath and flew into the glade. She loved how the force field tingled against her scales as she passed through it. Maybe it was her imagination, but she felt that the force field gave her extra power.

Once inside the glade, Mina paused to allow her eyes to adjust. In here, there was no green glow. Butterflies flittered about in the warm sunshine and birds twittered as if everything were perfectly normal.

But Mina knew things were far from normal in the rest of the forest. The memory of the Chaos Critters was still fresh in her mind. There had been so many of them. And they had definitely gotten bigger and stronger since the last time she'd encountered them.

Her twin and her cousin bounded over.

"Isn't this weird?" Hana said. "One minute we're playing online and the next, we're together in the Magic Forest."

"It's totally weird. But also totally great," Zora said. "I wish traveling was this easy back home."

Mina was about to agree when the majestic tree in the center of the glade began swaying back and forth. Mina knew what this meant: the Tree Queen was appearing!

A moment later, the tree transformed into an elegant woman. She was dressed in a soft moss-green gown, her long brown hair cascading over her shoulders.

"Welcome back, Storm Dragons," the Tree Queen said, smiling warmly at the three Storm Dragons. "I am very grateful to the three of you for repairing the Thunder Maker on your last visit. After that, things were calm here in the Magic Forest—for a time! But as I suspected, it wasn't long before the Chaos Queen worked out another way to wreak havoc." The Tree Queen sighed, her branches swaying. "Now she's targeted the Lightning House."

The Dragon Girls exchanged a look. *Lightning House?* Was that anything like a lighthouse?

"The Lightning House is the second weather station in the Magic Forest," the Tree Queen explained. "It's where lightning is created, to go with the thunder that's made by the Thunder Maker. It's vital that our lightning functions properly. Without healthy storm patterns, the harmony of the entire forest is affected. Our storms become dangerous."

The Storm Dragons loved a good storm. But they did not like dangerous ones!

"This is bad," growled Hana.

"Really bad," agreed Zora, her eyes wide.

"What has she actually done to the Lightning House?" Mina asked. Her mind had already switched into problem-solving mode. But first she needed to know exactly what had happened.

"At the top of the Lightning House are three

powerful orbs," the Tree Queen replied. "These orbs constantly rotate, beaming out bolts of lightning during a storm. Lightning is an important part of our storms, and it is also a power source for some creatures in the forest. But the Chaos Queen has stolen the orbs. When the Lightning House is attacked, a warning glow covers the forest. You have probably noticed it."

The three Storm Dragons nodded.

"It's bad enough that she has taken the lightning orbs," the Tree Queen continued. "What's worse is what might happen next. We fear she is going to use them to power her own evil plans. Tell me, Storm Dragons—did any of you witness strange lightning on your way to the glade?"

All three Storm Dragons nodded.

"It was green," Hana said.

"And it was all knotted," Zora added.

"Also, when the lightning appears, there's a weird buzzing sound," Mina finished. "It's like . . . static electricity."

"Then my suspicions are correct," the Tree Queen said. "The Lightning House orbs are extremely powerful. The Chaos Queen is surely going to use them to damage the Magic Forest and the lives of everyone who calls the forest home. That chaotic lightning and buzzing is no doubt terrifying the forest's creatures."

Hana looked like she was about to lose her temper. "We've got to stop her!" she cried, flapping her wings and rising into the air. "Now!"

The Tree Queen's serious face softened for a moment. "It's wonderful that you are so eager, Thunder Dragon."

Mina was used to her sister's fiery outbursts. Hana was so brave. Mina often wished she were more like that. But she'd always been the quieter, more careful twin.

The Tree Queen turned to Mina. "Lightning Dragon, today I am putting you in charge," she said. "This quest requires care, and great speed. These are your strengths. Here, take this and wear it around your neck. It will help you on your journey."

The queen stretched out a branch-arm. Dangling from a chain was what looked like a thermometer. But Mina knew better. This was the find-o-meter that they'd used on their previous quest.

Gratefully, Mina slipped the silver chain around her neck.

"She's changing back," Zora whispered sadly.

The elegant leader had indeed begun turning back into a tree.

Mina gulped. She didn't feel ready to set off on this mission. They needed more information!

Her twin clearly agreed. "Where should we start?" Hana asked the queen quickly, before it was too late.

"Head for the Lightning House," the Tree Queen replied, her voice sounding more woody with every word. "It's high on the pink cliffs, overlooking the Rocky Sea."

"Where's that, exactly?" Mina asked.

The Tree Queen's voice could just be heard through the rustling leaves. "You will know it when you see it. Trust your instincts."

The three Storm Dragons rose into the air and flew back through the force field.

"Am I imagining it or is the glow greener than before?" Hana asked as they headed off, flying between the dense trees.

"I think it is. And that buzzing feeling is

stronger," Zora said. "It's like how the air feels just before a massive storm."

Mina could feel it, too. Her scales tingled, and a high-pitched crackle rang in her ears. The sound grew until suddenly the sky lit up with chaotic squiggles of lightning. For a moment Mina saw birds and squirrels and other animals cowering on the branches of the trees, eyes wide with fear, before the green-tinged darkness descended again.

Like the Tree Queen had said, the creatures of the forest were frightened by the green lightning.

"We've got to find the Lightning House as soon as we can!" Mina called to the others.

"Absolutely," Zora agreed. "But how?"

Mina looked at the find-o-meter. She gave it a shake. Nothing. Was it broken?

"Maybe we should start flying in one direction and see if the find-o-meter responds?" suggested Hana, neatly ducking around a tree. "That's pretty much what we did last time."

Mina shook her head. Unlike her sister, she liked things to be planned out. She needed a reason to head in a particular direction.

"Let's fly above the tree line," she suggested. "Maybe we'll be able to see which way to go from up there."

Together, the Dragon Girls rocketed upward until they were well above the trees. The Magic Forest stretched out below them like a mysterious velvety carpet, glowing faintly yellow green.

"Any strikes of inspiration, Mina?" Hana asked, flying up beside her.

They're waiting for me to choose which way to go! Mina thought. It felt like a lot of pressure. Then she remembered what the Tree Queen had said. *I just need to trust my instincts.*

Right now, Mina's instinct was to think carefully about which way to go. She scanned the forest, looking for anything that might give her a clue. Far away on the horizon, she spotted something jutting out of the treetops. It was tall and silver and shaped like a zigzag.

Was that the Lightning House? It certainly looked like a lightning bolt.

Mina checked the find-o-meter again. It still hadn't moved. But all the same, Mina had a strong feeling this was the right way to go. Maybe she could be a little more like Hana, just this once.

"Follow me!" said Mina, flapping her wings and setting off toward the distant structure.

Even though Mina was worried about the quest, she couldn't help enjoying herself as they flew. It felt great to streak across the sky, dragon power surging through her. She zipped this way and that. Just how fast could she go?

Mina suspected the answer was *very* fast! She surged forward.

"Hey! Don't leave us behind." Hana laughed.

"Do you think we're close now?" Zora said a few minutes later, sounding a little winded.

Mina peered into the gloom and saw the silver zigzag shape was nearly below them. At the top were three long metal rods, reaching into the sky. At the end of each was a claw. Mina was puzzled. What where those things? Then it dawned on her. The claws must normally hold the three orbs! This was definitely the Lightning House!

It perched right on the edge of a tall cliff made of pink stone, just as the Tree Queen

had said. A sea of pink boulders stretched out before it, surrounded by the thick forest.

"Oh! I didn't know the Rocky Sea was literally a sea of rocks," Mina said.

"You never can tell in the Magic Forest," Zora commented.

Swirling around the Lightning House was a mass of clouds constantly shifting and changing.

"There's something strange about those clouds," Hana said, narrowing her eyes to look more closely.

"They're not clouds at all," Mina realized. "They're moths! Let's go and ask if they know what's going on. Maybe they can help us."

The Dragon Girls swooped down toward the chaotic cluster of insects.

"Are you sure they're moths?" Hana asked. "They're huge!"

"And they've got such pretty markings on their wings," Zora added. "Silver zigzags, like lightning strikes. I've never seen moths that look like that."

"True. But we didn't know we could look like dragons until recently," Mina pointed out. "Moths are attracted to light. Maybe these Zigzag Moths are flying in that odd way because the orbs are missing."

"Can you hear that noise?" Hana asked.

The moths were letting out high-pitched, worried sounds. As she approached, Mina could make out actual words.

"Three moons gone!" one moth cried, zigzagging past Mina.

"Bad. Very bad," moaned another, crashing into the first but not noticing. It zigzagged back in the other direction.

"Can't survive!" shrieked another.

The moths flew around and around, colliding with one another and abruptly changing directions, only to crash into other Zigzag Moths.

"They must call the orbs *moons*," Mina said.

"Of course!" said Zora. "And it seems like they really need them!"

"What they really need are traffic lights," muttered Hana, narrowly dodging two moths who were both moaning, "Catastrophe!"

Mina watched the Zigzag Moths swirling around. How was she going to get their attention? She flew right into the middle of the swarm and spoke clearly.

"I know you're worried about the missing, er, moons," she said slowly and carefully. "We think the Chaos Queen and her critters took them. Can you tell us anything about what happened?"

"Words hard!" cried a moth. "Flutter in brains! Green lightning and buzzing make worse!"

Mina's mind raced. Any information these

moths had would be so handy. But she could see that they were too confused and distressed to speak clearly.

When she was little, Mina sometimes had trouble finding the right words for her feelings. When that happened, she would draw pictures to show how she felt inside.

"Is there another way you can explain it to us?" she asked. "A way that doesn't use words?"

Excitement rippled through the moth community. Quickly, they arranged themselves so their wings formed a flat rectangle. Their beautiful patterns faded to black. A moment later, images began to move across the screen of wings.

Mina and the others watched a scene appearing on the moths' wings. They saw the tall silver shape of the Lightning House, glimmering against a dark sky. The claws on the metal rods held three bright lights, which turned slowly. *The orbs!* thought Mina. As they turned, the orbs sent bright, crackling bolts of electricity into the sky. Zigzag Moths fluttered happily around the light.

"Oh, lovely moons!" the moths crooned in delight.

Suddenly, a dark mass appeared.

"Chaos Critters," growled Hana, who was watching beside Mina.

"This must be when they steal the orbs," Zora predicted.

Sure enough, the squeaking mass of critters swarmed up and over the three orbs of light. Up close, Mina could see that the claws gripping the lights were carved like dragon talons, sturdy and strong.

"Look," said Mina. "The critters are biting at the claws!"

Her whole body felt tense. Whatever the critters were doing, it was not good.

To her dismay, Mina saw the talons slowly unfolding, creaking in protest as they did so. On the screen, the moths flew around in a panic, moaning and flapping their wings frantically.

"What is happening? Help! Help!"

"What's that light?" asked Hana, pointing to a glow to the right of the wing screen.

"Is it the sun rising?" Zora wondered, peering closer.

Mina shook her head. While the glow was

bright, it had a harsh coldness to it. From the center of the glow a woman emerged, dressed in swirling robes that sparked with electricity. She reached out from under her electrical cloak and lifted an orb from the now-open claw.

Mina watched in horror as the light faded from the orb—and flowed into the figure! Then the woman fastened the now-dull orb to her cloak with a chain of pure electricity.

"The Chaos Queen!" Mina gasped as the woman reached out and took the second orb, again draining its brightness. "It must be her. And she's draining the orbs of their power!"

Hana and Zola stared at the figure, too, their eyes wide. Mina could tell they were thinking the same thing as her: *How would they beat this evil queen?* She literally surged with power!

We'll find a way, Mina told herself. She just wasn't sure how yet.

On the moth-wing screen, the Chaos Queen snatched up the final orb in her long fingers.

Then, with her cloak sparking and buzzing with power, she whirled away, the faded orbs floating behind her on their electric leashes. Chattering and squeaking loudly, the Chaos Critters scampered back down the tower.

The Lightning House scene faded from the screen. Mina leaned forward, holding her breath. Would the image reappear? It was vital to know what happened next. Luckily, a moment later a new scene appeared.

Mina could see the critters scuttling down something pink toward a vast stretch of rocks. High above, the Chaos Queen zipped through the sky like a comet.

"So, the Chaos Queen flew over the Rocky

Sea," Mina said. "And the critters climbed over the edge of the cliff and followed their queen."

"To the Rocky Sea, then!" Zora said.

"Hang on," said Mina, holding up a paw to silence the others. "The Chaos Queen is talking."

"Keep going, my Chaos Critters!" called the queen. "I'll meet you—"

The image disappeared again. And this time, it didn't return.

"Agh!" Hana moaned. "That's so frustrating!"

Mina felt the same way. They *really* needed to know where the Chaos Queen planned to meet her critters!

"Can't remember more," explained the moths

sadly, flapping their wings so their normal zig-zag pattern returned.

"Maybe we can replace the drained orbs with new ones?" Zora suggested.

"That might work," agreed Mina.

After all, this was what they did at home when a light bulb blew. And the Dragon Girls had managed to get a new Thunder Drum made last time they were in the Magic Forest to fix the thunder.

"Unfortunately, the lightning orbs cannot be replaced," Gleami explained, suddenly appearing by Mina's side. "The orbs are as old as time, and the secret of how to make them was lost long ago."

The Storm Dragons looked at one another and nodded. Mina and Hana often had the same thought at the same moment. But this time, all three Dragon Girls knew exactly what they needed to do. If the orbs couldn't be replaced, they had to be found and returned.

As one, they flapped their wings and rose into the air.

The moths began flying around in panicked circles. "Where go?"

"Don't worry!" called Zora. "We'll find the orbs—I mean, moons."

"And we'll bring them back safe and sound," Hana promised. "Won't we, Mina?"

Mina nodded, but inside her head, her

thoughts swirled. She really, really hoped they could pull this off!

The noise of the Zigzag Moths quickly faded as Gleami and the dragons sped away from the Lightning House and over the edge of the pink cliff. Mina's mind raced. What if the orbs had already been smashed onto the rocks? Was the Chaos Queen planning to destroy them?

As they flew, Mina noticed the buzzing noise again. She could feel it all through her body. It was like when the dentist cleaned her teeth—but worse. Soon, the buzzing was so intense Mina could hardly admire the shiny pink Rocky Sea stretching out below them.

"I feel jittery," muttered Hana.

"Me too," said Zora. "I'm all jangly and mixed up."

"I feel it as well," said Mina. "I think the Chaos Queen's chaotic energy is affecting us. Let's try to keep flying. Maybe we can push through it."

But the powerful feeling showed no sign of fading. Normally Mina found it easy to stay calm and focused. But right now, it was as though there was a warning siren in her head, mixing up her thoughts.

"Watch out, Mina!" whispered Gleami in her ear.

Mina looked down to see a swarm of Chaos Critters surging over the rocks below. Surely they were too far away to be of danger? There were no trees for the critters to climb up, after all. Even the tallest rocks didn't reach anywhere near where the Storm Dragons were flying. But this did not matter. Mina gasped in dismay as, letting out earsplitting shrieks, the critters leapt high into the air.

"Dodge them!" Mina yelled. But it was too late. With bloodcurdling screams, the Chaos Critters landed on the Storm Dragons. Mina could feel their dreadful little claws clinging to her, crawling up her back and along her tail. She shot a look at Hana and Zora. They, too, had the awful critters swarming over them.

“As the Chaos Queen’s power grows, so does the power of her Chaos Critters,” cried Gleami. “Mina, you must get them off you as quick as you can.”

“You need to roll or shake the critters off!” Mina called out to the others, trying a mid-air spin herself. This got rid of some creatures, but she could feel others gripping on, their claws digging in around her tough scales. She rolled the other way, tucking in her wings and spinning faster and faster until she was dizzy. She righted herself and tried tumbling forward, lashing her tail from side to side as she somersaulted.

More critters fell off, screeching angrily. But a few were still clinging on. Usually Mina was good at problem-solving. But it was much harder with her ideas all jumbled up.

"I can't get them off me," Hana called.

"Me neither," Zora moaned.

Mina hated hearing the worry in her twin's and cousin's voices. She could see hundreds of Chaos Critters clinging to Hana's tail—not just with their claws but also with their teeth. And Zora's wings were covered so thickly it was clear she was having trouble flying.

Mina narrowed her eyes, sparks flaring from her nostrils. It was bad enough dealing with the Chaos Critters. But watching them attack two of her favorite people in the world was more than she could stand!

A rumbling started deep in her stomach. She was different from Hana and it took a lot to make her angry. But when it happened, Mina felt it strongly. And right now, she was very angry indeed.

Her fury grew and grew until a roar burst from her. Mina loved the feeling of dragon roaring. It was so satisfying to fill the air with such a loud, dramatic noise. But this roar was different. It sent bright flashes of light zigzagging into the air, fizzing with energy!

"Mina! You're roaring LIGHTNING!" Hana called, her eyes wide. "It's the coolest thing I've ever seen."

"And look! You scared off all the Chaos Critters on you!"

It was true. To her relief, Mina could no longer feel any of the creatures crawling over her. But the same wasn't true for Hana and Zora. Just looking at them covered in critters brought on a new flare of fury. Flapping her wings as hard as she could, Mina flew up close to the others. Her next lightning roar was so loud and so bright that it lit up the strange green sky for a moment.

As the brightness faded, Mina saw dark shapes falling from Hana and Zora. The annoying buzzing grew fainter and fainter, then stopped altogether. Finally, as the last of the Chaos Critters plummeted onto the rocks below, Mina found herself wrapped in a midair wing-hug.

"You did it!"

"Thanks so much! You're the best!"

"Anytime!" Mina laughed. "Now we should hurry. I want us to catch the Chaos Queen before she destroys the orbs. Plus, those critters might jump back on us if we don't get a move on."

The Storm Dragons surged forward, Mina leading the way. But where were they going, exactly? Mina had been checking regularly, but the find-o-meter still wasn't working. All Mina knew was that the Chaos Queen had stolen the orbs from the Lightning House, and then headed out over the Rocky Sea.

Mina looked down at the stretch of pink rocks below. They had been flying over the rocky landscape for a long time now. How big was the Rocky Sea? Was the Chaos Queen hiding behind a boulder somewhere, waiting to leap out and attack? And if she'd hidden the orbs, how were the Dragon Girls going to find them in this vast place?

"The orbs have their own special power," Gleami told her. "If they think you are trustworthy, they will send a signal to you."

Eagerly, Mina scanned the horizon, looking for a signal. All she could see were rocks and more rocks. But then, far away, Mina spotted something bright and swirly in the dark green sky.

"Is that lightning?" she asked Gleami.

"I don't think so," said Gleami. "There shouldn't be any real lightning without the orbs in place."

Mina wondered what to do. Should they check it out? Was this the signal? Or should they just keep looking for the orbs? She took a deep breath and tried to center her thoughts.

"I think we'd better check it out," Mina said.

The idea scared her a little, but at least she wouldn't be alone. Nothing is as scary when it's faced with friends.

She turned to the others, and instantly saw that something was very wrong with Zora. She looked like she was struggling to fly.

"What is it?" she asked her cousin, slowing so she could fly alongside Zora.

"I'm not sure," said Zora, wincing with each wing flap.

"The critters must have injured her wing," Hana said.

"I'm fine," Zora insisted, but she was clearly in a lot of pain.

Mina thought hard. She knew they needed to check out the lights on the horizon, but she wanted to look after Zora, too.

"Maybe I could have a quick rest?" Zora asked. "I'm sure I'll be fine in a moment."

"Definitely. Let's get you down onto the pink rocks," Mina said as she began to form a new plan. She would leave her cousin to rest and ask Hana to take care of her. As for Mina, she would go and investigate that strange lightning. Alone.

Mina was not quite alone, of course. Faithful Gleami zoomed along beside her. Something about the steady hum of Gleami's wings made Mina feel less nervous about exploring by herself. The glowing on the horizon loomed brighter as she approached. The streaks of light were as fast and white as lightning bolts, but they didn't disappear like lightning. Also, they were moving in a swirling pattern, almost like birds circling prey.

As Mina and Gleami flew on, Mina noticed the pink rocks below changing size. She had left Zora and Hana resting on huge boulders. But gradually the rocks were shrinking—first to the size of stones, then down to pebbles. A little farther on, they dissolved into very fine pink sand.

"It's salt," Gleami explained.

But Mina didn't reply. She had noticed something about the strange lights moving in the sky. "They're not lights at all. They're alive! Look, Gleami. They've got eyes—and teeth. Big teeth!"

"Yes! I can see they're Electric Sky Eels," Gleami replied, her own eyes wide with wonder. "I've heard about them, of course. They're famous. But I've never seen them. They only appear during electrical storms, or when the Magic Forest is dangerously out of balance. Maybe they've appeared now because the orbs were removed? It's said they are very bright, but not always very helpful."

"Why is that? Aren't they friendly?" Mina asked, a little nervously. The closer they got, the stranger the eels looked. Their long bodies flashed as they wriggled and squirmed through the air, sending out shimmering sparks behind them.

"I hear that they're slippery and hard to pin down," Gleami said.

Mina nodded. Slippery made sense for an eel. *But I'll find a way to get the help we need,* she told herself.

She flapped her wings harder than ever, determined to get over to the eels as soon as possible. But whenever she got close, the creatures seemed to wriggle farther away.

"Please stay still for a moment!" Mina called out. "We need your help."

"We ARE helping," called one of the eels. "You just don't realize it. Keep your wits about you, Lightning Dragon, and you will see the light."

Mina could not understand how the eels wriggling away from her was helping. But before she could say anything, another flash of green, knotted lightning ripped across the sky. It was so bright that Mina turned her head away from the glare. And that was when she saw something glowing very faintly below her, half-buried in the pink salt.

Mina hovered over the spot, her eyes fixed on the gleaming shapes below.

"They look like huge light bulbs," Mina said, her heart thumping. "Gleami, are they the missing orbs?"

Gleami's wings buzzed with energy. "Yes! They look like they've lost most of their power, which isn't great. But the important thing is, you've found them. Good work!"

"See? We told you we were helping," called the eels, who were now doing loops and circles through the air. "We led you to the orbs."

"Thanks," Mina called back politely. "But... well, it would have made this a lot easier if you'd just *told* me where they were."

"Ah, but we don't like to do things the easy way," the eels replied, flicking trails of sparks into the air. "We like to do them the eely way."

Mina wished Hana and Zora were there with her to hear this. The dragon way was much simpler than the eely way, in her opinion!

"Now you've found the orbs, how will you rescue them?" asked the Electric Sky Eels.

"I'll just fly down and pick them up, I guess," Mina replied. It seemed like a strange question.

"It's not so simple, Lightning Dragon," replied the eels. "You're one dragon, and yet there are three orbs. We eels can't help. No hands! Your gleaming friend there has six hands, but none of them are strong enough to hold an orb."

Mina paused. The eels were making a good point. The orbs were much bigger than she'd expected. How would she carry all three of them at once? In the scene they'd watched on the moths' wings, the Chaos Queen had attached the orbs to a belt with electric chains. But Mina didn't have anything like that.

"I wonder if I can balance them somehow," Mina said.

"Better grab them quick, then, before the salt grabs you!" called the eels, whirling and twirling and laughing.

Mina looked at Gleami. "What do they mean?"

"It's hard to say. Electric Sky Eels speak in slippery riddles." Gleami sighed. "But I fear it's not safe to rescue the orbs alone. We should probably go back and get the other Storm Dragons."

Mina hesitated. It was tempting to have her twin and cousin by her side. But what if Zora's wing was still injured? And what if Mina couldn't lead them back to this very spot? The Rocky Sea was huge, the glow of the orbs faint, and she wasn't sure she could rely on the eels to stay in place to help her navigate.

Mina tensed as the buzzing reverberated all through her. Green lightning flashed again, brighter than last time. That decided it for Mina: The Magic Forest was in danger and it was her job to protect the forest and return the orbs. After all, she was the Lightning Dragon.

She took a deep breath. "I'll be quick as a flash," she promised Gleami.

"I don't think you should do this," Gleami warned. "I sense danger!"

But Mina knew she had no choice. Tucking her wings in close, she dove. She reached out her talons, ready to lift the orbs out of the salt and fly straight up into the sky again. But when she wrapped her talons around an orb, it would not budge. *I'll have to dig it out*, Mina decided.

Mina landed lightly. As soon as her feet touched the salt, the eels whipped through the air in a web of light. "Get off!" they cried. "You're standing on quicksalt!"

Mina tried to scramble free, but it was impossible. With every movement, she felt her paws slipping into the fine pink salt, pulling her down, down, down.

Mina froze, her entire body rigid. She knew that with quicksand, the more you moved, the deeper in you sank. But even though Mina was not moving at all, she could feel herself being dragged deeper into the fine pink powder.

"Quicksalt is different from quicksand," Gleami explained to Mina, fluttering anxiously overhead. "It's not moving your body that pulls you down. It's whirling thoughts. You must try to calm your brain. Even better, don't think at all."

Don't think? That was impossible. Even thinking about trying not to think made Mina slip farther into the quicksalt. What was she going to do?

Then, in the distance, Mina heard a sound. This time it wasn't that awful buzzing. It was dragon roars! Joy rushed through her. She knew who those roars belonged to.

"Don't worry, Mina," Hana called in her booming voice. "We'll get you out of there!"

"Is your wing okay, Zora?" Mina called, feeling herself slip lower as worries about her cousin flittered through her mind.

"It's much better," Zora called back, sounding like her normal, cheerful self again. "Resting it really helped. Which is lucky because it looks like we got here just in time."

"When you get here, don't land on the ground!" Mina warned as her twin and cousin grew closer.

Thoughts burrowed into her brain, no matter how much she tried to keep them out. Like, what would happen if Hana and Zora landed by accident? Or what if they couldn't get her out? Mina kept sinking lower. Even worse, the three orbs were sinking with her!

Once again, Mina tried to blank out her mind. But that just seemed to lead her to more thinking about how bad she was at not thinking about, well, everything.

"Close your eyes," Gleami urged, still hovering beside her. "And listen to the sound of my wings."

Mina closed her eyes as instructed and listened. Slowly, a sense of calmness washed over her as she focused on the gentle, even buzzing of Gleami's wings.

To her relief, her slide into the quicksalt stopped.

Then she heard different wings, these much bigger and stronger. They were beating right overhead. Opening her eyes and looking up, Mina saw the most wonderful sight. Hana and Zora were there, grinning down at her!

"Ready for us to pull you out?" Hana asked.

Mina nodded, then felt herself slip down a little deeper as a thought crashed into her head. "Don't forget the orbs! We need to get them out of the quicksalt, too."

Hana swooped down on one side of Mina, Zora on the other. They hooked their back paws under Mina's wings, grabbing an orb each in their front paws. Mina clasped on to the third one.

Hana and Zora flapped their wings, hard. But no matter how hard they tried, they couldn't pull Mina out!

"Something is weighing you down," Hana puffed.

Oh no! This isn't going to work! Mina thought, her mind spiraling again. Instantly, she felt herself sliding lower into the quicksalt.

"Don't panic," Gleami reminded her. "Remember, you can trust your sister and cousin."

The moment Gleami said that, Mina felt her worries drop away. Gleami was right. *Of course* Hana and Zora would get her out of there. The Tree Queen had told her to trust her instincts. And right then, Mina's were telling her that her sister and cousin would stop at nothing to save her.

"Hey!" Hana cried. "You're lighter all of a sudden."

"And look at the orbs!" Zora called.

As Mina watched, the three orbs rose up and out of the quicksalt on their own. Moments later, Mina's wings were free of the quicksalt. Then, with a few powerful flaps, Mina managed to pull herself out entirely.

"Woo-hoo!" she shouted, so thrilled to be unstuck that she started zipping this way and that through the air, gripping the orb tightly in her front paws.

"What's gotten into you?" Hana laughed as Mina zoomed by, looping and spinning.

"It's not what's gotten into me, it's what I've gotten out of!" Mina grinned.

"It's amazing that you found the orbs, Mina," Zora said.

"Sure is," Hana said. But then she frowned at the blank orb she was carrying. "Except they are so faint now that the Chaos Queen has taken their power. I wonder if we can get it back from her somehow."

"Impossible!" called the Electric Sky Eels, who were still circling above. "It's like trying to put juice back into an orange."

But Mina wasn't worried. Her mind felt so clear after being released from the quicksalt. Instead of having a thousand half thoughts, she had a single clear one: *Find a way to fix the orbs.* "Do you know how we can charge the orbs with fresh power?" she asked.

"That's eely," the eels replied. "We can recharge them. There's only one catch."

Hana groaned. "Why is there always a catch?"

"You have to catch us first!"

With that, the eels took off, trailing bright, crackling sparks behind them.

"After them, quick!" Mina cried. She was determined not to let these slippery eels slip away!

Together, the Storm Dragons tore across the dark, green-tinted sky after the eels. As the eels weaved this way and that, they left a stream of light behind them. Mina and the others stuck close as the eels led them higher and higher before plummeting toward the Rocky Sea. Then, at the very last minute, they pulled up.

Wherever the eels went, the dragons kept pace, flying right behind them. They were so close, Mina could feel the sparks from the eels' tails fizzing and popping against her scales.

Zora, who was at the back of the group, gave a shout of surprise. "Look at the orbs!"

Mina's heart jumped. Had something bad happened to these precious objects? She had been so focused on not letting the eels out of her sight, she had almost forgotten about the orbs.

But nothing was wrong with the orb she was holding. In fact, it had begun to glow. She glanced over at Hana and Zora, and a huge smile crept across her face. The orbs they were carrying were glowing, too!

It dawned on Mina what was happening. "The light trails from the eels are recharging the orbs!"

"Of course they are," called the eels, laughing as they slowed down, looping back and forth. "We said that all you had to do was catch us and they would be charged. It was obvious."

Mina saw Hana roll her eyes and tried very hard not to laugh. The eels were certainly a little tricky to deal with. But the three orbs were glowing brightly now thanks to them, so Mina wasn't going to complain!

"We really appreciate your help," she said politely.

The eels whirled about, streaking the sky with their fiery trails.

"Happy to help, Storm Dragons," said one. "After all, we are depending on you to return the forest's storms back to normal. We get our energy from lightning bolts."

"But this weird green lightning doesn't power us at all," said another eel. "It actually leaves us hungrier. The quicker you can fix things, the better. We love storms."

The Storm Dragons certainly agreed with the eels on this. There was nothing quite like a good storm!

Mina and the others began to flap their wings at full force. Roaring goodbye to the eels, they took off back to the Lightning House. Mina was at the front, silhouetted against the green glow of the horizon. Gleami fluttered faithfully by her side, and Hana and Zora were close behind.

As they flew, the fine pink salt below them grew coarser. It turned to pebbles, then rocks, then boulders. As the stones grew, so did Mina's nerves. She wasn't sure why. They had found the orbs and managed to recharge them. Now all they had to do was return them to the Lightning House. Why was she worried?

Mina thought back to the Tree Queen's comment about just being herself. Maybe she was right to be nervous. *I'll keep my guard up*, she thought.

Green lightning crackled, illuminating the sky. The lightning was only brief, but it was enough for Mina to spot something very strange. The moths were fluttering above the Lightning House in a huge cloud, but their wings were flashing bright red. Mina heard Hana and Zora gasp.

"It looks like the moths are trying to warn us about something," Mina said softly.

"They're much more helpful when they use their wings instead of their words," Zora whispered back. "Maybe the Chaos Critters are nearby?"

Mina nodded. "I bet the critters are expecting us to fly straight to the top of the Lightning House to return the orbs," she said under her breath. "I say we do the complete opposite."

"What do you mean?" Hana asked.

But there was no time to explain. "Follow me and fly as low as you can. They'll be scanning the skies for us. Let's stay out of their sight."

Mina, Hana, and Zora swooped down low, barely skimming the boulders of the Rocky Sea as they approached. When they reached the cliff, they hugged close to it, using their sharp talons to climb. At the top, they slunk over as quietly as they could. Mina was out of breath but excited. The Lightning House was just ahead, and there was still no sign of the Chaos Critters. All the same, Mina could sense they were close.

So could Gleami. "Be very careful," she whispered. "The eels might not feed on that green lightning but the Chaos Critters do. They will be bigger than ever. And angrier."

The huge heavy door at the base of the Lightning House silently opened as the Storm Dragons drew near. Despite the danger, Mina couldn't help smiling. It was as though the building itself was on their side, helping them avoid the pesky Chaos Critters! Mina tucked the orb under her wing and stepped through the doorway.

It was dark inside, but the glow from Gleami's wings and the orb allowed Mina to see a staircase. It zigzagged back and forth as it led up. At the top of the tower, Mina spied the underside of a trapdoor. Very faintly she could hear the scratching sounds of Chaos Critters as they scurried around.

"The trapdoor leads to the roof," whispered Gleami in her ear.

Yes! This was exactly what Mina was hoping for.

Hana and Zora came in quietly behind her. "Are we going to sneak up there and surprise the critters from the inside?" Zora asked softly.

Mina nodded. "They'll be watching the skies, waiting for us to appear. They won't think to look down."

At least, I hope they won't, thought Mina.

"I promise I'll be quiet," Hana said.

"Actually, you can be as noisy as you like," Mina assured her twin. "We're going to roar up a storm that blows those critters right out of here."

Hana laughed. "I like the sound of that!"

On the count of three, the Storm Dragons

flew up the stairs, roaring at the top of their lungs. Mina's roar sent electric sparks flying. The sparks bounced wildly off the zigzagging walls. Hana's roar was always loud, but in the Lightning House it seemed to double in volume. And Zora's roar was a mighty, icy blast, which whirled around the space, carrying sound and the lightning sparks with it.

From high above came screeches of shock. The critters' claws scuttled furiously as they prepared for battle.

But the Storm Dragons were already prepared. At the top of the stairs, they roared again, using their power to burst through the

trapdoor. The air shimmered with the combined force of sound, electricity, and ice, sending the critters tumbling into the gloomy night.

Gleami clapped two of her wings together like she was clapping hands. "Well done, Storm Dragons!" she cried.

But Mina was not ready to relax just yet. Before her, illuminated by the glow of the orbs, were the three tall rods, their empty claws stretched open and waiting.

Mina steadied herself for a moment. The buzzing sound was building again, which meant more lightning was coming. *Focus, Mina*, she told herself. They didn't have much time—she could already hear the critters scrambling back up the tower. She needed to get this right.

She turned to Hana and Zora. "I'm going to roar as loudly as I can. Hopefully that will hold off the critters while you get your orbs back into their rightful positions. Ready?"

"Ready!" came the reply.

Mina drew in a big breath. Summoning all her power, she let out her hugest roar yet.

Bright flashes of light shot about as Mina's roar lit up the sky. The sound drowned out the annoying buzzing. Mina felt power coursing through her.

"Go!" she roared to Hana and Zora, shooting out more flares of light.

Mina saw the remaining few Chaos Critters

scuttling away as fast as their scratchy little legs could carry them.

Zora went first, fitting her orb into the first open claw. Instantly, the metal talons closed tightly around the orb.

Hana went next, placing her orb into the second claw. Once more, the sharp metal talons gripped the shining orb.

My turn, thought Mina. Mina flapped her wings and leapt toward the third claw. Gently but firmly, she pushed the final orb into position. With a snap, the claw took hold of it.

Mina landed back down between her sister and cousin.

"Did we do it?" Zora asked. "I'm waiting for something dramatic to happen."

"I'm not sure," Mina admitted.

"I have a feeling there's something else we need to do," Hana said.

Immediately, Mina knew her twin's hunch was right. The orbs were in place, they were glowing with power, but they weren't spinning like they had in the moths' movie.

"The orbs need to be activated," Gleami explained.

"Let's all roar?" Mina suggested.

Together, their roars filled the air! As she roared, Mina thought about the Chaos Queen. How dare she steal the orbs and suck their power! She was putting the Magic Forest at risk, just to make herself stronger.

Mina felt her fury turn into pure energy as she roared again. Thick streams of crackling light lashed the air, glowing white hot. With an enormous crack, the streaks zigzagged down to the three orbs, zapping them. The orbs flashed and, very slowly, they began to spin. Their light shot out of the tower and into the forest beyond.

"It's working!" Hana whooped.

Zora gave Mina a wing-hug. "All thanks to you, Mina," she said.

"Are you kidding?" said Mina. "I would still be stuck in quicksalt if it wasn't for you two. We did this together."

There was a loud crack as lightning flashed across the sky. But this lightning wasn't acid green and knotted. It was a perfect zigzag, as clear and bright as lightning should be. And a moment later, thunder rumbled.

"Just like a real storm." Hana sighed happily.

"And look! This is finally working again," said Mina, holding up the find-o-meter. The silver line was no longer frozen in place.

"Hey, what's that?" Zora pointed.

High above, tiny explosions of color filled the sky. Sparkling dots drifted down like fireworks. In between the sparks were flutters of white, zigzagging this way and that. With each direction change, the fluttering things changed color.

"It's the Electric Sky Eels and the Zigzag Moths," Mina said. "What are they doing, I wonder?"

"Maybe they're putting on a show for us,"

Hana suggested. "To say thanks for fixing the lightning?"

"Or maybe they're just happy," Zora said, shrugging.

"Could be both," Mina said. "Or it could be for a completely different reason. It's very hard to tell with eels and moths."

Hana and Zora laughed in agreement.

Gleami fluttered closer. "Sorry to cut the celebration short, but it's time to return to the glade. The Tree Queen wants to see you before you go home. I can lead you there, or would you rather use the find-o-meter, now that it's working again?"

"You lead the way, please," Mina said. The find-o-meter was a cool device when it worked, but nothing was as cool as a dragonfly with glowing wings!

With a final glance at the wonderful, bright lightning orbs, Mina, Hana, and Zora followed Gleami through the dark night sky.

As they made their way back through the

Magic Forest, the storm continued to build. Thunder rumbled and lightning crashed as they flew. Mina couldn't stop smiling. There was something very special about flying through a storm she'd helped create.

Clearly, Mina wasn't the only one enjoying the weather! Despite the darkness, birdsong rang out and Mina saw forest creatures running below, leaping delightedly. A group of tiny bunnies gathered at the base of a tree as the Storm Dragons flew by, waving their little paws up at them. "Thanks for fixing the lightning!" they squeaked.

"No problem!" Mina called back.

Although it had been a huge quest, Mina

didn't feel at all tired. In fact, she had more energy than ever. She was almost sad when she saw the glow of the Tree Queen's glade below. She wanted to keep flying forever.

"Don't worry," said Gleami, seeing her disappointed expression. "I have a feeling you'll be called back into the forest before long. I think the Tree Queen has more to ask of you."

Mina nodded happily. "I'm sure we'll be back."

She thanked the beautiful dragonfly for all her help, then whooshed through the shield protecting the glade with her sister and cousin. Mina dropped neatly onto the grass beside Hana and Zora.

Mina looked around. The glade looked even more lush and welcoming than before, if that was possible. The colors seemed brighter, the air fresher.

The sound of rustling leaves filled the glade, and soon the tall tree in the center transformed into the Tree Queen.

Her eyes sparkled as she looked at Mina, Zora, and Hana. "My dear Storm Dragons! You have done wonderfully well," she said in her kind way. "This quest was particularly tricky. I knew you would succeed, of course, but you showed very impressive speed and intelligence throughout."

Mina felt like she was glowing from within. Praise from the Tree Queen was the best!

A more serious look came over the Tree Queen's face. "However, as you may have guessed, the battle with the Chaos Queen is far from over. You have done so much for the Magic Forest already. Are you prepared to come back once more?"

That was an easy question to answer. "Of course!" Mina, Hana, and Zora cried together.

Mina held out the find-o-meter. "The chaotic lightning stopped this from working for a while, but it seems to be okay now. Maybe we can use it next time?"

The Tree Queen nodded as she took back the find-o-meter. "Thank you, Lightning Dragon. The Chaos Queen's power is growing. Now that she has orb energy, she will be stronger than ever. I suspect the Magic Forest will need you to return very soon. As before, my signal will be a storm in your world. But keep in mind, there are many different types of storms!"

What does that mean? Mina wondered. But she decided not to ask. It would be fun to wait and find out!

The Tree Queen began to sway. A mist filled with twinkling lights rose and swirled around the glade, making everything within it fade away.

"Goodbye, Storm Dragons," called the Tree Queen through the dazzling haze. "Until next time."

Mina closed her eyes, feeling the mist curl around her. When she opened them again, Mina was back at home, sitting at her kitchen table. The storm was dying down. Her mom's laptop was open and she was still logged into *Magic Treasure Zone*. As she stared at the screen, the chat lit up.

How amazing was that?! Hana wrote.

So amazing! Zora responded. *Hey, I've got to log off. See you soon!*

Mina leaned over the keyboard. *Really soon!* she typed. *In the meantime, let's watch out for storms!*

Turn the page for a special sneak peek of

Zora's adventure!

Zora pressed her nose against the cab's window, her excitement growing. She recognized this street. It was just around the corner from her cousins' house. This weekend, Zora's mom had to travel for work to the city where Hana and Mina lived. And she'd taken Zora with her!

Zora and her mom had gotten up very early that morning to catch the plane, but Zora didn't mind. She kept thinking about how surprised her cousins would be to see her. Hana and Mina had no idea Zora was coming to stay for two nights. She couldn't wait to see their faces!

"This will be the second time you've seen your cousins this year," Zora's mom said, reaching over to squeeze her hand. "First at your grandma's birthday, and now this trip."

What Zora's mom didn't know was that the cousins had seen one another even more than that. And not just in the games they played together online. Recently, the three girls had been called to a mysterious place called the

Magic Forest. While there, Zora, Hana, and Mina transformed into magnificent Storm Dragons and went on important quests.

Her cousin Hana was the Thunder Dragon. She had a little cloud on her forehead. Mina was the Lightning Dragon. On her forehead was a zigzag shape, just like a bolt of lightning.

It made perfect sense to Zora that her cousins were thunder and lightning. They were twins, so they really belonged together. But at the same time, they were very different. Just like thunder and lightning!

When Zora transformed into a dragon, she had a snowflake on her forehead. She liked snow a lot. It was so fun to play with. She also loved how snow blanketed the world, making everything calm and quiet. Looking out the window and discovering that it had snowed overnight was the best way to wake up, in Zora's opinion.

Just then, Zora saw a white fleck float by the cab's window. Then she saw another and another. Snowflakes!

"Look at that sky," Zora's mom said. "It's gone completely white. A snowstorm is on the way."

Zora had to stop herself from gasping. The ruler of the Magic Forest—the Tree Queen—had told Zora, Hana, and Mina to look out for storms. Could this snowstorm really be a message from the queen that it was time to return?

Excitement pulsed through Zora. Could it be time to return to the Magic Forest? She really hoped so!

By the time they pulled up outside the cousins' house a few minutes later, snow was falling thick and fast. The wind had picked up, sending white flakes whirling. Zora and her mom gathered their bags and hurried up the driveway. It was very cold. Zora was glad to have the new hat her mom had bought her.

Zora rang the doorbell, her heart beating so fast she thought she might burst. She loved visiting her cousins. Their house was always full of people, pets, and noise. Mostly, Zora preferred things to be organized—but it was so fun to visit the mayhem of her cousins' home!

"What?!" Mina cried when she opened the front door. "It's so great to see you! What are you two doing here? Hang on, come in out of the cold before you answer that. Watch out for our art project. It's kind of taken over the house."

Zora and her mom were ushered into the warm, messy, friendly home. They were soon joined by Hana, a dog, two cats, and Zora's aunt and uncle. Everyone was talking, barking, and meowing at the same time as they made their way down the hall and into the kitchen.

"We're making hot chocolate," Hana explained. "But not normal ones. We thought we'd add a bit of chili."

"And then we're going to stir in some ice cream right at the end," Mina added. "What do you think?"

Zora laughed. She didn't want to be rude, but she would rather skip the chaotic ingredients and stick to the normal recipe.

"Come on," Hana begged. "Let's mix things up. We might create an amazing new taste."

Zora was about to say that she didn't think chili and ice cream would be good in hot chocolate when she noticed something. Her hat was missing.

“My hat! I must have dropped it outside,” she said.

“That’s not like you,” said Zora’s mom. “You’re usually so careful with your things.”

“You’ve caught our messy gene already,” Hana joked.

“You can run, but you can’t hide,” added Mina, wiggling her fingers dramatically.

“You two keep your messiness away from me,” Zora joked back. “I’ll just go and find my hat.”

“Be quick,” Zora’s mom said. “This storm is getting worse by the minute.”

Zora, Hana, and Mina exchanged a look. Clearly they were all wondering the same thing: Was this storm their signal from the Tree Queen?

"I will," Zora promised, dashing back down the hall and out the front door.

Outside, the snow was so thick that Zora could barely see a few feet ahead. Sheltering her eyes with her hand, she looked around the driveway. Ah! There was her hat. As Zora took a first step toward it, she heard singing.

Magic Forest, Magic Forest, come explore . . .

This song was familiar to Zora. She'd heard it both times she had been called into the

Magic Forest. Zora grinned to herself. She was going back! Carefully, she took another step, her foot sinking deep into fresh snow. As the snow whirled about her, the song grew louder.

Magic Forest, Magic Forest, come explore.

Zora reached out her arms, feeling the power of the wind and snow and eagerly listening for the final line of the song . . . the line that would transport her back to the Magic Forest. When she heard it, Zora joined in, singing pure and clear:

Magic Forest, Magic Forest, hear my roar!

Zora felt herself lift off the ground and spin around and around as the world faded to white.

The spinning stopped and Zora felt the ground beneath her once more. She looked down. Yes! She was back in dragon form! Zora loved how strong she felt as a dragon. She also loved knowing that with a few flaps of her powerful wings, she could soar into the air. It was so great to be back in the Magic Forest.

But hang on . . . Zora turned on the spot. Was she definitely in the Magic Forest? The landscape looked completely different from how it had the last time she'd visited. The colorful plants and lush grass were all covered with a layer of snow. *Blue* snow!

"Maybe snow is always blue in the Magic Forest," Zora said to herself.

Lots of things about the Magic Forest were unexpected and, well, magical.

But deep inside, Zora knew that there was something wrong. Sure, snow sometimes had a faintly blue look to it. But this snow was electric blue. It didn't look at all natural. When she scooped up a pawful, it even felt different.

Rather than soft and crunchy, it was rough and scratchy.

A little creature bounded toward her. It looked like a very fluffy fox. It was completely white except for the tips of its ears, which were pink. But unlike foxes in Zora's world, this one had wings growing from its back.

"This is not normal snow that you are looking at, Storm Dragon," the fox said.

ABOUT THE AUTHORS

Maddy Mara is the pen name of Australian creative duo Hilary Rogers and Meredith Badger. Hilary and Meredith have been making children's books together for many years. They love dreaming up new ideas and always have lots of projects bubbling away. When not writing, Hilary can be found cooking weird things or going on long walks, often with Meredith. And Meredith can be found teaching English online all around the world or daydreaming about being able to fly. They both live on the lands of the Wurundjeri people in Melbourne, Australia. Their website is maddymara.com.

DRAGON GIRLS

#1: Azmina the Gold Glitter Dragon

#2: Willa the Silver Glitter Dragon

#3: Naomi the Rainbow Glitter Dragon

#4: Mei the Ruby Treasure Dragon

#5: Aisha the Sapphire Treasure Dragon

#6: Quinn the Jade Treasure Dragon

#7: Rosie the Twilight Dragon

#8: Phoebe the Moonlight Dragon

#9: Stella the Starlight Dragon

#10: Grace the Cove Dragon

#11: Zoe the Beach Dragon

#12: Sofia the Lagoon Dragon

Collect them all!

DRAGON GAMES

PLAY THE GAME. SAVE THE REALM.

READ ALL OF TEAM DRAGON'S ADVENTURES!

Forever fairies . . . and forever friends!

READ THEM ALL!